Sports Superstars

MAX VERSTAPPEN

BY ETHAN OLSON

WWW.APEXEDITIONS.COM

Copyright © 2024 by Apex Editions, Mendota Heights, MN 55120. All rights reserved. No part of this book may be reproduced or utilized in any form or by any means without written permission from the publisher.

Apex is distributed by North Star Editions:
sales@northstareditions.com | 888-417-0195

Produced for Apex by Red Line Editorial.

Photographs ©: Robert Szaniszló/NurPhoto/AP Images, cover; Emilio Morenatti/AP Images, 1, 6–7, 8, 29; Shutterstock Images, 4–5, 10–11, 12, 13, 18–19, 20, 21, 22–23, 24–25; Eduardo Verdugo/AP Images, 14–15; Luca Bruno/AP Images, 16–17; Beata Zawrzel/NurPhoto/AP Images, 26–27

Library of Congress Control Number: 2023900329

ISBN
978-1-63738-561-6 (hardcover)
978-1-63738-615-6 (paperback)
978-1-63738-719-1 (ebook pdf)
978-1-63738-669-9 (hosted ebook)

Printed in the United States of America
Mankato, MN
082023

NOTE TO PARENTS AND EDUCATORS

Apex books are designed to build literacy skills in striving readers. Exciting, high-interest content attracts and holds readers' attention. The text is carefully leveled to allow students to achieve success quickly. Additional features, such as bolded glossary words for difficult terms, help build comprehension.

CHAPTER 1
A BIG FINISH 4

CHAPTER 2
EARLY LIFE 10

CHAPTER 3
FORMULA 1 STAR 16

CHAPTER 4
WORLD CHAMPION 22

COMPREHENSION QUESTIONS • 28
GLOSSARY • 30
TO LEARN MORE • 31
ABOUT THE AUTHOR • 31
INDEX • 32

CHAPTER 1

A Big Finish

It's the final **lap** of the 2016 Spanish **Grand Prix**. The race is close. Max Verstappen is in the lead. It's his first race for team Red Bull.

The 2016 Spanish Grand Prix took place near Barcelona, Spain.

Two other drivers close in on Verstappen. But he moves his car to block them. They don't have room to pass.

Formula 1 cars can drive faster than 200 miles per hour (322 km/h).

FORMULA 1

Grand Prix races are part of Formula 1 (F1). In this racing style, drivers use **open-wheel** cars. They compete in a series of races around the world.

Verstappen steers into the last turn. He presses the gas, and his car zooms ahead. He crosses the finish line in first place.

Fast Fact

Verstappen's win made him the youngest F1 driver to win a Grand Prix. He was 18 years old.

Max Verstappen celebrates after winning the 2016 Spanish Grand Prix.

CHAPTER 2

EARLY LIFE

Max Verstappen grew up in Belgium. Both his parents were **competitive** racers. They taught Max to race, too.

Max Verstappen was born in the city of Hasselt, Belgium.

Young drivers often start by racing go-karts, which are smaller than other cars.

Max began driving go-karts when he was only four years old. Soon, he was winning races and setting **records**. Max won his first kart **championship** when he was nine.

KART CHAMP

KZ is the top division of go-kart racing. It has the most-skilled drivers. When Max was 15, he became the youngest person to win its world championship.

There are several classes of go-kart racing. Drivers are divided by age and skill.

Max's skills got the attention of racing teams around the world. He joined Scuderia Toro Rosso in 2015. At 17, he became the youngest F1 driver ever.

Scuderia Toro Rosso had the same owners as Red Bull Racing. It helped young drivers get ready to move up to the top team.

FAST FACT
Max's father, Jos, also raced in Formula 1. He helped Max train.

CHAPTER 3

FORMULA 1 STAR

Max Verstappen raced with Toro Rosso for the 2015 **season**. Then he moved up to Red Bull Racing. That is one of Formula 1's top teams.

F1 teams have two drivers. In 2016, Red Bull's were Max Verstappen (front) and Daniel Ricciardo (back).

At the 2016 Malaysian Grand Prix, Verstappen (left) and Ricciardo (right) both reached the podium. They finished in second and first place.

Right away, Verstappen showed he belonged. First, he won the 2016 Spanish Grand Prix. Then he had six more **podium** finishes that season.

FAST FACT

Verstappen won Rookie of the Year after his first season in F1. This award goes to the best new driver.

Verstappen had 11 podium finishes during the 2018 F1 season.

By 2018, Verstappen was one of the best F1 drivers. He finished fourth overall that season.

COUNTRY CONNECTIONS

Max Verstappen competes as a Dutch racer. He grew up in a part of Belgium that's very close to the Netherlands. So, Verstappen feels attached to both countries.

Verstappen holds up the flag of the Netherlands.

CHAPTER 4

WORLD CHAMPION

Verstappen continued to improve in 2019 and 2020. He finished both seasons in third place. In 2021, he tried to place first.

Verstappen speeds past the crowd during the 2019 Austrian Grand Prix.

BECOMING CHAMPIONS

Teams and drivers collect points throughout each F1 season. The person with the most points at the end is the Drivers' Champion. The team with the most points wins Constructors' Champion.

By the last race, Verstappen was tied for first with Lewis Hamilton. Hamilton led for most of the race. But Verstappen sped ahead in the final lap. He became the 2021 Drivers' Champion.

In each Formula 1 race, the top 10 drivers get points for their positions.

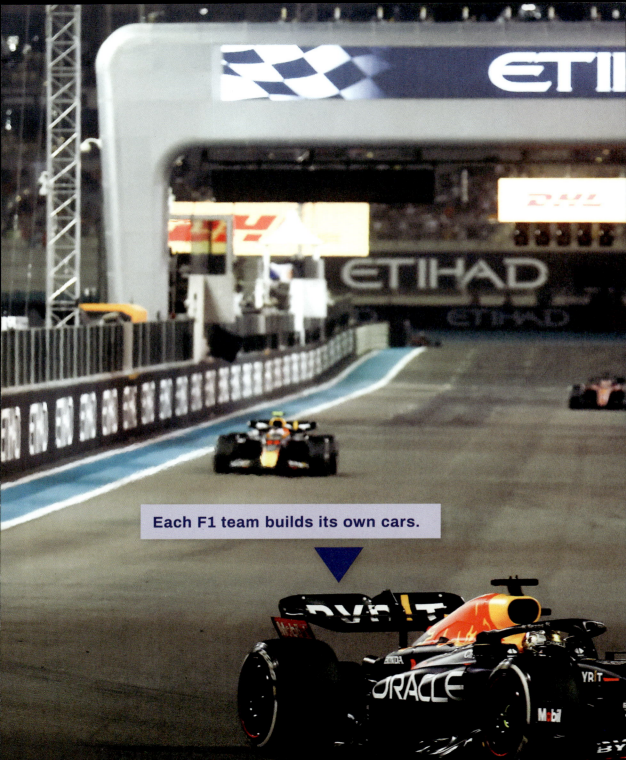

Each F1 team builds its own cars.

Verstappen was Drivers' Champion again in 2022. Red Bull was the Constructors' Champion, too. Fans looked forward to more great races.

FAST FACT
In 2022, Verstappen broke the record for most wins in one season.

COMPREHENSION QUESTIONS

Write your answers on a separate piece of paper.

1. Write a few sentences describing the main ideas of Chapter 2.

2. Would you rather drive a go-kart or a Formula 1 car? Why?

3. Which F1 team did Verstappen first join?
    - A. Red Bull Racing
    - B. Scuderia Toro Rosso
    - C. Constructors' Champion

4. How many podium finishes did Verstappen have during his first season with Red Bull?
    - A. one
    - B. six
    - C. seven

5. What does **division** mean in this book?

KZ is the top division of go-kart racing. It has the most-skilled drivers.

- **A.** racetrack
- **B.** group of drivers
- **C.** kind of car

6. What does **attached** mean in this book?

*He grew up in a part of Belgium that's very close to the Netherlands. So, Verstappen feels **attached** to both countries.*

- **A.** stuck
- **B.** connected
- **C.** angry

Answer key on page 32.

GLOSSARY

championship
A contest that decides a winner.

competitive
Taking part in events where people try to win games or sports.

Grand Prix
A car race that takes place on a long, difficult course.

lap
One loop around a racetrack.

open-wheel
Having wheels on the outside of the car.

podium
The place where drivers stand after winning first, second, or third place in a race.

records
Best or fastest performances.

season
The series of Formula 1 races that take place around the world each year.

BOOKS

Cain, Harold P. *Lewis Hamilton: Auto Racing Star*. Lake Elmo, MN: Focus Readers, 2023.

Gish, Ashley. *Formula One Cars*. Mankato, MN: Creative Education, 2021.

Rule, Heather. *GOATs of Auto Racing*. Minneapolis: Abdo Publishing, 2022.

ONLINE RESOURCES

Visit **www.apexeditions.com** to find links and resources related to this title.

ABOUT THE AUTHOR

Ethan Olson is a sportswriter based in Minneapolis, Minnesota. He is dedicated to sports but also enjoys making music and exploring nature in his free time. He'd love to cover a World Cup one day.

INDEX

B
Belgium, 10, 21

C
Constructors' Champion, 24, 27

D
Drivers' Champion, 24, 25, 27

F
Formula 1 (F1), 7, 9, 14, 15, 16, 20, 24

H
Hamilton, Lewis, 25

N
Netherlands, 21

R
Red Bull, 4, 16, 19

S
Scuderia Toro Rosso, 14, 16
Spanish Grand Prix, 4, 19

V
Verstappen, Jos, 15

ANSWER KEY:
1. Answers will vary; 2. Answers will vary; 3. B; 4. C; 5. B; 6. B